Alcohol Is a Drug, Too

What Happens to Kids When We're Afraid to Say No

David J. Wilmes

JOHNSON INSTITUTE®
Minneapolis

Alcohol Is a Drug, Too
What Happens to Kids When We're Afraid to Say No

Johnson Institute
7205 Ohms Lane
Minneapolis, MN 55439-2159
(612) 831-1630 or (800) 231-5165

Library of Congress Cataloging-in-Publication Data

Wilmes, David J.
    Alcohol is a drug too / David J. Wilmes.
        p. cm.
    ISBN 1-56246-057-9
    1. Teenagers—United States—Alcohol use. 2. Parent and teenager—United States. I. Title.
HV5135.W56   1993
362.29' 17' 0835—dc20
                                   93-9574
                                   CIP

Cover design: LightSource Images
Text design: Mark Stefan

Printed in the United States of America.
94 95 96 97 98 / 5 4 3 2 1

Acknowledgments

- Thanks to the parents, educators, and concerned adults I've had the opportunity to meet and talk with. Your commitment to your kids is a constant source of inspiration for me.

- Thanks to all of the Johnson Institute staff. Your behind-the-scenes hard work, dedication, and creativity reflect a passion for excellence that is second to none.

- Thanks to the Miller Family Foundation of Stone Mountain, Georgia. Your enlightened support has helped thousands of parents learn to make a difference in their kids' lives.

- Most of all, thanks to Connie, Scott, and Michael. Your love and hugs at the end of the day makes everything worthwhile.

Contents

Introduction

1

As a community of adults—parents, teachers, business people, police officers—our most cherished prize is our children. We've sacrificed for them; we've invested in them; we've spent sleepless nights worrying about them. They are our future, our dreams. In some ways, they are us.

When harm threatens our children, we unite to defeat the foe. We do whatever is necessary to guarantee their safety and to assure them the opportunity for a better life.

In the past fifteen years, drugs have become an important threat to our children. When we think about drugs, many of us primarily think about cocaine, crack, heroin, and other illegal chemicals. In the past five years, crack cocaine has in fact come to exemplify the enemy in our nation's "war on drugs."

We have progressed in our effort to prevent the use of many drugs. Unfortunately, however, some of us have unintentionally implied that alcohol is less dangerous than other drugs we have identified as "the enemy" and that it may even be safe for our kids to use.

Consider the evidence regarding alcohol:

- As a drug, alcohol resembles anesthetics: it depresses the central nervous system. Historically, alcohol was used to dampen the sensation of pain for surgical purposes, until the late nineteenth century when ether, nitrous oxide, and chloroform were discovered.

Alcohol use plays a significant role in numerous injuries and violent acts involving young people. Consider the following statistics:

- Alcohol-related traffic crashes are the leading cause of death and spinal cord injuries for young Americans.[1]

- On average, an alcohol-related traffic death occurs every twenty-three minutes in the United States.[2]

- A study of homicide victims in Atlanta, Georgia found that over 50 percent had blood alcohol levels of .10 percent or greater.[3]

- In a survey of students at a southwestern university, 55 percent of sexual assault perpetrators and 53 percent of sexual assault victims admitted to being under the influence of alcohol at the time of the assault.[4]

- A 1990 survey of Massachusetts adolescents between the ages of sixteen and nineteen found that 49 percent reported being more likely to have sex if they and their partner had been drinking.[5]

- Researchers in Pennsylvania found a striking association between the ingestion of alcohol and the use of firearms as a method of suicide. They conclude that the epidemic increase in the suicide rate among youth may be associated with an increase in the prevalence of alcohol abuse.[6]

- Two distinct studies have found that from 40 to 50 percent of young males who have drowned or sustained diving injuries had consumed alcohol immediately prior to the incident.[7]

- In a national survey, college administrators estimated that student alcohol use leads to 69 percent of damage to residence halls and is responsible for 34 percent of academic problems on U.S. campuses.[8]

A young participant in a 1992 conference on alcohol-related injuries and violence cited the U.S. Surgeon General's statistics: 10 million high school students in the United States have engaged in alcohol abuse. An estimated 27 percent of those have driven while intoxicated. "Alcohol drinking creates a domino effect," the student went on to say:

> It leads to many other problems including increased rates of fires, homicides, suicides, sex crimes, child abuse, and motor vehicle crashes. Alcohol must no longer be looked upon as an individual problem. We must target specific groups and speak to them. Society as a whole needs to redefine alcohol as a drug; one that can be fatal.[9]

We adults must prepare ourselves to become as educated and single-minded as the young student. By continuing to dismiss and minimize the dangerous impact of this drug alcohol, we join in the dangerous game of denial.

What Questions Confront Us?

Many questions confront us as we consider underage use of alcohol:

- As adults, how do we teach kids about this drug, alcohol?

- How can we prepare them for the reality that they will legally be able to use this drug at a certain age?

- Isn't it a double message that adults over a certain age can drink but young adults cannot?

- What can we do when our children tell us that all their friends drink, many with their parents' approval?
- Won't we be peculiar if we take a firm stand against alcohol use by young people?
- What do we do about the "peer pressure" we adults experience—pressure to let kids drink or to look the other way when they drink?

One reality is clear: even though we have made progress in preventing young people from using certain drugs, the consequences of the underage use of alcohol have increased. The casualties linked to underage use of alcohol are on the rise. In fact, alcohol use and its related consequences are the number one health risk to adolescents and young adults today.

No simple solutions to this problem exist. We will make a life-saving impact only by facing the problem squarely and taking responsibility for our part—whether we're parents, educators, police officers, pastors, or business people.

The goal of this book is to encourage the process of thinking and talking in families, schools, religious congregations, and chambers of commerce, about how we can all begin to face this critical issue.

Basic Beliefs About Alcohol and Young People

Before you go any further, please take a few minutes to stop and reflect on what you really believe about alcohol use by young people. Consider each of the following questions. If possible, jot down your responses or a few key words that reflect your thoughts. Remember, these reflect only your opinions and thoughts.

1. Why do young people drink?

_____

_____

2. What attitude should young people have toward alcohol?

_____

_____

3. What information do young people need about alcohol?

_____

_____

4. What concerns do I have about underage drinking in my city, community, or family?

_____

_____

A Checklist of Opinions

Parents, educators, and other adults have made the following list of statements about young people and their use of alcohol. Think about each statement and note whether you agree, disagree, or are undecided about it.

	AGREE	UNDECIDED	DISAGREE
1. Alcohol use is a positive rite of passage. Preventing kids from drinking is an attempt to prevent their growing up.	❏	❏	❏
2. Communication is the real issue. Kids who have open communication and family support will not develop alcohol or other drug problems.	❏	❏	❏

	AGREE	UNDECIDED	DISAGREE
3. Kids will use alcohol regardless of what *any* adult says or does.	❏	❏	❏
4. Beer and wine coolers are relatively safe for kids. Kids get in trouble only when they use the hard stuff.	❏	❏	❏
5. The best way to teach kids about alcohol is to let them try it. Let them take sips when they are younger. Let them try a small glass of wine with the meal as they reach their teen years.	❏	❏	❏
6. I know my adolescent uses alcohol occasionally. But if I confront her about her use, I will only push her further away. Ignoring her use is the best way to go.	❏	❏	❏
7. Adolescents can't become chemically dependent—they're too young.	❏	❏	❏
8. Alcohol doesn't cause nearly the number of problems for our culture as other drugs, such as crack or cocaine.	❏	❏	❏
9. Laws and rules that prohibit underage drinking don't work. Kids will never accept the fact that adults can do it but kids can't.	❏	❏	❏
10. Adults' use of alcohol has no impact on kids. Kids look only to their peers as role models.	❏	❏	❏

Each of the above statements reflects the opinions and feelings of many who are trying to sort out beliefs regarding underage use of alcohol. *Each of these statements, however, is false.*

Even though the ten statements are false, they are extremely important because they raise the issues that prevent us from giving our children a clear, no-use message about alcohol. The fact is that many adults base their feelings and opinions about underage drinking on falsehoods.

Facts Regarding Underage Drinking

Fact 1. *Allowing underage kids to use alcohol does not instill in them a sense of maturity or responsibility.*

It can be healthy for young people to play-act adulthood. Pretending to be older by renting a tuxedo at prom time or making independent decisions regarding clothing and hairstyles can be very positive. Unfortunately, when we allow underage kids to play adult by using alcohol, the results are destructive. In fact, alcohol consumption is associated with irresponsibility. Research from Johnson Institute *StudentView*® indicates that a correlation exists between parental permissiveness in their youngsters' use of alcohol and unacceptable behavior exhibited by those youngsters.[10] When parents allow underage kids to use alcohol for any reason (other than religious services), the young person is two times more likely to engage in anti-social behavior, e.g. getting into fights, stealing, or vandalism.

Fact 2. *Neither we nor our children are immune to alcohol or other drug problems.*

Research indicates that young people who feel they have family support and open communication are less likely to develop problems with alcohol or other drug use. However, family support does not work like a vaccination against problems. Even children from families where parents have been open and supportive have developed serious problems with alcohol or other drugs.

Fact 3.   *Adult opinions (especially parents') significantly affect young people's decisions to use or not use alcohol and other drugs.*

Young people's decisions about alcohol or other drug use are based on a variety of factors. The Minnesota Student Survey conducted in 1992 found that, among high school students who do not use alcohol or other drugs, their second most popular reason for abstinence is that their parents would be upset. The fact is that adult opinions do influence young people's decisions about alcohol and other drug use.

Fact 4.   *Beer and wine coolers are the most common alcoholic drinks that create problems for underage drinkers.*

Parents and young people sometimes view beer and wine coolers as "safe" forms of alcohol. However, they are not safe. One twelve-ounce beer or six-ounce serving of wine contains as much alcohol as one ounce of distilled alcohol, such as gin, whiskey, or vodka.

Unfortunately, this "safe" reputation has led to very high levels of use by young people. In *Youth and Alcohol: A National Survey,*[11] the U.S. Inspector General reports that 35 percent of all wine coolers sold in the U.S. are consumed by junior and senior high school students. Fifty-one percent reported wine coolers as their favorite drink because they like the flavor and they think wine coolers do not contain much alcohol. One of three students did not know that all wine coolers contain alcohol.

Particularly dangerous are fruit-flavored fortified wines, which often contain as much as 20 percent alcohol. Because these fortified wines have such high alcohol content and resemble wine coolers, the U.S. Office of the Inspector General reports that a number of alcohol-related deaths, especially among youth, have been tied to this form of alcohol.

Fact 5. *Allowing kids to use alcohol even under adult supervision gives young people a double message.*

Data from Johnson Institute's *StudentView*® research tells us that adolescents whose parents permit their alcohol use for any reason other than religious services are three times more likely than their abstaining classmates to develop serious problems with alcohol or other drugs.

The research is quite clear that all adults—parents, educators, police officers, and others—must consistently oppose young people's consumption of alcohol.

Fact 6. *Adults who ignore underage drinking become part of the problem.*

Unfortunately, many adults "overlook" underage drinking, thus tacitly giving approval. Consider the following data from the U.S. Office of the Inspector General:

- Two-thirds of the students surveyed who use alcohol report they are able to buy alcohol on their own.[12]

- Three-fourths of the seventh graders who drink report getting alcohol from their parents.[13]

- One-third of state law enforcement officials believe that public indifference makes the control of underage drinking difficult.[14]

Fact 7. *Kids can and do become chemically dependent.*

Johnson Institute's *StudentView*® data reports that as early as ninth grade, 5 percent of our young people are experiencing multiple problems directly related to their use of alcohol and other drugs. They are at risk of chemical dependence. By eleventh grade, 10 percent of the students surveyed meet criteria that put them in the chemical dependence group.

Fact 8. *Alcohol is a dangerous drug.*

According to the U.S. Department of Health and Human Services, "Alcoholic beverages are the most widely used, enjoyed, and abused addictive substance in America. They exact one-and-a-half times the health cost and three times the economic damage of tobacco....[Alcohol use] is responsible for one in twelve fatalities, on an average of more than 570 deaths per day.[15]

The cost of alcohol problems in America was recently estimated at $70 billion per year. All other drug use combined was estimated to cost $44 billion annually.[16]

Fact 9. *Laws and rules have an impact on young people's behavior only if we enforce them in a way that actually affects youth rather than their parents.*

The U.S Office of the Inspector General interviewed state law enforcement officials and found that "...traditional, statutory penalties do not deter youth. Judges rarely sentence minors to jail, and parents usually pay the monetary penalties, not the minors."[17]

Twenty eight states have found that delay, suspension, or revocation of young people's driving licenses, however, does deter underage drinking. As one official noted, "The one thing that a minor cares about is his driver's license."

Diversion programs such as community service work coupled with counseling for the youth and education for the parents have also been effective deterrents.

The fact is that laws do deter young people from using alcohol and from developing serious problems associated with alcohol use. We must, however, enforce the law in a way that has direct impact on the young person.

The U.S. Department of Transportation estimates that "Since 1975 minimum drinking age laws have saved at least 10 thousand lives."[18]

Fact 10. *Adult behavior has a significant impact on kids.*

Research from Johnson Institute's *StudentView*® and other research data tells us that adolescents whose parents have problems related to alcohol or other drug use are three to four times as likely to develop such a problem themselves. While peers do affect students' immediate choices, the fact is that parents and family factors are significantly more powerful in determining which young people will develop alcohol or other drug problems.

Adults need accurate information in order to develop informed opinions about the use of alcohol by young people. With solid facts to guide us, we can prepare our kids to deal with the dangers and risks associated with alcohol.

Acting on Falsehoods 2

Most people either accept many of the myths listed in Chapter One or are undecided about them. Accepting that all ten statements are false is not easy. This chapter provides some specific examples of what happens when adults act on these false beliefs about alcohol.

Falsehood One

Illicit drugs, such as crack, cocaine, L.S.D., and so on, pose a much greater threat to kids than alcohol does. To keep kids off these illicit drugs, it's okay to overlook the occasional use of alcohol. *This belief is false.*

Acting on the Falsehood

Bob Helmers works for the police department. He has seen firsthand the consequences of illicit drugs like cocaine on some of the addicts the police bring into the station.

Because Bob realizes how dangerous and addictive these drugs are, he wants to be sure that his own kids never touch any of this stuff. So he's made a deal with his sixteen-year-old son, Stan. He's agreed to overlook occasional use of alcohol if Stan obeys certain conditions: he drinks only beer, he drinks only at home, and he never drinks and drives.

Bob's decision is based on two beliefs: he can't keep his kids away from alcohol, and certain illicit drugs are much more dangerous than alcohol. Bob is familiar with alcohol. He has an occasional drink now and again. He feels fairly confident that any danger from drinking beer wouldn't be much of a problem.

Impact

Bob has actually increased his son's chances of using the very drugs he is most concerned about. He has also introduced his son to the dangerous consequences of the drug, alcohol.

Bargaining doesn't work. Kids whose parents allow them to use alcohol for any reason are

- more likely to use illegal drugs such as cocaine, marijuana, and L.S.D.;

- more likely to develop serious dependence problems with alcohol and other drugs;

- and more likely to experience dangerous consequences (legal problems, medical problems, relationship problems, or personal problems) as a result of alcohol or other drug use than are kids who report that their parents take a firm no-use position regarding alcohol.[1]

Falsehood Two

Drinking is okay for kids as long as they never drink and drive. *This belief is false.*

Acting on the Falsehood

Sylvia Olson is a driver-education instructor. She routinely teaches both underage and older students, providing behind-the-wheel and classroom instruction to prepare them for their driver's license exam. In her classroom instruction, she uses a video that dramatizes the fatal consequences of drinking and driving.

Now that her oldest daughter is sixteen, Sylvia's professional concern has become personal. She has told Lorna not to drink and drive. When Lorna goes out with her school friends, Sylvia always asks to be sure that one of the friends is the designated driver for the evening.

Impact

Sylvia Olson is giving Lorna tacit approval to drink. Her daughter has heard the following message: "Drinking is okay; just don't drink and drive." Sylvia is communicating to her daughter the expectation that if a sober teenager is designated to drive the car, the other underage youth will probably use alcohol.

This assumption transmits a dangerous message to young people. When parents allow their kids to use alcohol for any reason, the young person is more likely to drink and drive and more likely to be in a car driven by someone who has been drinking than are young people who report their parents take a firm no-use position regarding alcohol.[2]

Sylvia Olson has good intentions; unfortunately, she's operating with information that is only half true. Drinking and driving is deadly for kids. Permissiveness with alcohol is *not* a deterrent.

Falsehood Three

Problems with alcohol and other drug use develop only in unhappy families. As long as we love our kids, everything will be fine. *This belief is false.*

Acting on the Falsehood

Reggie Conners teaches parent education in the adult enrichment program in his church. He also volunteers his time as a lay counselor, providing support to other adult members of his congregation. In his parent education program, he routinely skips the section on alcohol and other drug use because he assumes that no one in his church has that kind of problem. After all, the members of his congregation are all "good people."

In the past six weeks, however, Reggie has been counseling a family who are having problems with their seventeen-year-old son, Tim. Reggie repeatedly suggests that the parents focus their attention on maintaining open and supportive communication with Tim and that they ignore his use of alcohol. Reggie maintains that Tim's use of alcohol is only an attempt to get attention. If his parents give Tim enough attention and love, alcohol won't be a problem.

Tim's parents shake all of Reggie's beliefs when they tell him that, based on an assessment following his second arrest for driving under the influence, the court has ordered Tim to undergo treatment for chemical dependence.

Impact

Reggie became a co-conspirator in Tim's drinking problem. By diverting attention away from Tim's drinking problem, he sent the message that alcohol use is "no big deal."

Despite our best intentions, we cannot inoculate anyone against problems related to the use of alcohol or other drugs. Not even beloved members of our family, school, or community are immune to problems with alcohol or other drugs. These problems cut across all race, economic, and religious groups.

While open communication and support from the family are essential to the healthy growth and development of young people, these benefits provide no guarantee that young people will never develop drug problems. Reggie gave poor advice when he advised Tim's family to ignore his use of alcohol in order to maintain a friendly and cordial flow of communication.

Falsehood Four

Underage drinking is normal for kids. We adults only create more problems when we make a "big deal" out of drinking. *This belief is false.*

Acting on the Falsehood

Frank Smits is a neighborhood police officer. While patrolling the neighborhood park last night, he ran into three ninth-grade kids with a six-pack of beer. Each of them had already drunk one beer.

Technically, Frank knew he should take the young people to the station, call their parents, and refer them to the juvenile first-time offender program. However, the kids pleaded with him not to tell their parents. He knew a lot about family violence. Could their parents be violent? He didn't want to cause problems for the kids or for their parents.

So Frank decided to give the kids a break. He poured out the remaining beer, gave the three ninth-graders a firm lecture about alcohol and other drug use, and sent them home. He hoped the kids got the message and appreciated the break he'd given them.

Impact

These three kids got a message but it wasn't the one Frank wanted them to hear. What they understood from this encounter was that the police do not consider the drinking of alcohol by underage kids a serious matter.

The kids experienced no consequences for their actions. Both children and adults learn from the consequences of their behavior. By attempting to be understanding, Frank communicated a very dangerous message: drinking alcohol is okay.

Adult permissiveness regarding underage drinking always leads to more drinking.

Falsehood Five

Kids are too young to become alcoholics. *This belief is false.*

Acting on the Falsehood

Sol Salberta coaches the varsity basketball team. Nathan, his star center, has been a loyal player ever since he was in ninth grade. During the past year, however, Nathan hasn't been himself. His performance on the team isn't what it used to be; his personality seems to be changing; and he's more irritable, upset, and difficult to get along with. Sol has heard that Nathan is drinking a lot, that he goes to a lot of parties, and that he has some problems. In fact, one of Nathan's best friends recently told Sol that Nathan was having blackouts. (A blackout is a temporary memory loss following heavy use of alcohol.)

Sol dismisses these rumors because he believes that Nathan is too young to develop a problem with alcohol. Moreover, Sol thinks that changes in Nathan are rooted in his anxiety about choosing the college where he's going to play basketball. Having received two scholarship offers, Nathan faces a tough decision. Sol figures that, once Nathan makes his decision about college, he'll be okay.

Impact

Nathan gets the message from his coach that everything is okay. By dismissing the obvious clues that something is wrong, Mr. Salberta misses an important opportunity to help his student.

Young people *do* develop problems with alcohol and other drug use. Statistics indicate that as many as 10 percent of high school seniors like Nathan exhibit problems that put them at great risk to become chemically dependent on alcohol or other drugs.

Ignoring the signs of teenage alcoholism only worsens the problem and delays assistance to adolescents when they really need it—before a tragedy takes place.

Falsehood Six

Kids today have all the solid information they need regarding alcohol and other drugs. They wouldn't be interested in hearing an opinion from an adult about this topic.

Acting on the Falsehood

Brenda Dobson owns a Dairy Queen that employs eighteen young people nine months a year. They are the backbone of her work force. Lately she has noticed that Maria, one of her best employees, isn't herself. The girl occasionally comes to work late and looks tired and run-down.

Brenda also notices that a new crowd picks up Maria after work. Other workers say that Maria's new friends are heavy drinkers.

Brenda knows the impact of friends on other kids. She worries that the influence of Maria's new friends may be hurting her. Even though she wants to talk about this concern with Maria, Brenda hesitates. Assuming that the girl knows what she's doing and doesn't want input from an adult, Brenda withholds feedback that Maria needs to hear.

Impact

Like Mr. Salberta, Brenda's reluctance to speak up to her employee results in a lost opportunity. Too many young people have no adult in their lives who could guide them or provide accurate information.

In a recent survey of over 20 million students, the Office of the Inspector General found that over 9 million students have received their information about alcohol from unreliable sources. More than 5 million students say they "just picked up" what they know by themselves or that no one has taught them about alcohol.

The same survey clearly indicates that young people who do not drink are much more likely to have learned about alcohol from an adult than are their peers who drink. Teenagers who drink report that their primary source of information about alcohol is friends, themselves, or nobody.[3]

Brenda's invalid assumption that Maria isn't interested in adult feedback prevents Brenda's providing help and support. Maria needs all the input she can hear from adults like Brenda. The perspective of teachers, employers, and parents really does make a difference.

Summary

False assumptions about alcohol cause adults to withhold the mature viewpoint and the guidance teenagers need. When that appropriate relationship between youth and their elders breaks down, adults become part of the problem.

From the silence of parents, teachers, police officers, pastors, employers, and others, we communicate to young people that underage alcohol use is not really a problem. We communicate, often without saying anything, that underage drinking is acceptable. Unwittingly, we *enable* teenagers to harm themselves with the powerful drug, alcohol.

Enabling: Good Intentions, Bad Results

3

Many of us glimpse ourselves in the anecdotes about adults who turn a blind eye to teenage drinking because we too have enabled young people to use alcohol. Oftentimes, we did so because we were attempting to help or because we wanted to avoid conflict.

Enabling often means something positive—empowering others to prosper. The enabling that unwittingly allows and sometimes even encourages kids to use alcohol or other drugs, however, is destructive to them. We harm them by shielding them from the consequences of their decisions and actions.

A Father's Enabling

The example of Bill and his seventeen-year-old son, Mark, clarifies this concept.

Bill is a single parent. Two strong feelings plagued Bill for six months, while he had custody of Mark: he felt responsible for the breakup of his marriage, and he felt guilty about the effects of the divorce on his son.

Mark's counselor from his new school recently called Bill to report inconsistent attendance and conflicts between Mark and other students that on occasion had escalated into a fight. The counselor suggested referral for private counseling or at least the assistance of school support groups that helped students appropriately resolve conflict.

The counselor believed that Mark needed additional support and a consequence clearly related to his recent skirmish on school grounds. However, either option required parental notification and approval before Mark could receive counseling.

Bill disagreed with the counselor. He felt that Mark's only problem was his difficult adjustment to a new school. To single him out as a "nut case" by putting him in a group or in therapy would only make it harder for him to find friends. Bill believed that Mark deserved a break. After all, his parents had just divorced and he was new in this school. The problem, as Bill saw it, was that everyone expected too much from Mark. The young man only needed time to make friends and adjust.

After talking to the counselor, Bill decided that Mark didn't need therapy, he needed a car. How did Bill arrive at this decision? Well, Mark claimed that he hadn't made any new friends because he didn't have a car and so could not socialize with other kids. (Mark actually didn't have a car because he had never been able to save the money for a down payment or insurance.) Because he was out of town, Bill had missed Mark's seventeenth birthday. Bill also had been thinking that he needed a new car himself. Why not buy a car and give Mark his old one?

Within a month, Bill had bought a new car and turned over the keys of his three-year-old Ford to his son. Excited and thrilled, Mark promised to work harder at school and assured his dad that everything was going to be better.

Bill had a business trip coming up in two weeks. He would be on the West Coast for three days and wouldn't be home until Saturday afternoon. Mark said that, because of his car he had made several new friends; he wanted to invite them to a party while his dad was gone.

Bill had reservations about this plan. He'd heard about the loud parties that had disrupted the neighborhood. But after all, Mark had had trouble making friends and adjusting to a new school. Maybe a party *was* the way for Mark to connect with his new friends.

So Bill gave in and allowed the party. He gave Mark two guidelines: only ten or twelve kids could be at the party and it had to break up by midnight. Bill was still unsure, but he wanted to show Mark that he trusted and loved him.

On Friday night, while Bill was still on the West Coast, he received a phone call at 3 A.M. When he picked up the receiver, he heard Mark sheepishly say that the police had arrested him and two friends for possession of alcohol. He was calling from the police station. The other parents had already come and taken his two friends home.

Bill was outraged. His immediate reaction was to blame the police. *Don't the police have anything better to do than be on the prowl for these kids who are just being kids?* he asked himself.

Bill's second reaction was to blame the neighbors who called the police. *Can't they be a little more understanding?* he wondered. Eventually Bill blamed his son's peer group. According to Mark, a number of uninvited troublemakers started a fight with Mark and his new friends. Mark had invited only a few kids, but the party expanded beyond his control. Yes, he and his friends had been drinking a few beers, but no one had said they couldn't.

Bill called the attorney who had represented him in his recent divorce. He was sure some legal maneuvering could rescue his son

31

from the new problems he faced. After all, he was a good kid caught in a difficult situation that really wasn't his fault.

The Results of Enabling

The story of Bill and Mark illustrates an enabling relationship between a son and a parent who intends only to help. Enabling is usually done for good reason and from the best of motives. Most of us enable because we really want things to turn out right for our kids. Often we enable because we are trying to fix a problem for them or make up for our own feelings of guilt or inadequacy as parents.

Unfortunately, enabling doesn't help. In fact, it hurts. By enabling, we actually encourage our kids, or at least allow them, to be irresponsible. We shield them from the consequences of their decisions and actions.

Let's reflect on Bill and Mark's story. How did this father enable his son to be irresponsible? Reread the story and find at least two examples that demonstrated enabling. Also note Bill's reasons for enabling his son and jot down your thoughts below:

Bill enabled Mark by _____

_____

I suspect the reasons for Bill's actions were _____

_____

A second way Bill enabled Mark was _____

_____

I suspect Bill's reasons were_____

_____

Bill enabled Mark in a number of ways. His enabling was sometimes directly related to alcohol use and sometimes to other kinds of behavior.

Enabling Example

Action: When the counselor suggested outside counseling or involvement in the school support group, Bill shielded Mark from this natural consequence of his behavior.

Reason: Bill really believed that Mark only needed more time to make friends. Also he took responsibility for Mark's behavior because he felt guilty about his recent divorce.

Result: Mark heard the message that if he skipped school or fought at school, his Dad would get him out of the jam.

Enabling Example

Action: When the police arrested Mark for unlawful possession of alcohol, his father hired an attorney in an attempt to get the charges dropped.

Reason: Bill felt guilty because he had been out of town for three days and left Mark alone. He believed that the school, police, and neighbors were scapegoating his son, thinking that Bill was a poor parent.

Result: Mark received a second message. This one told him that even if he broke the law, his dad would fix everything for him.

How to Detect Enabling

Bill and Mark's story suggests the complexity of the enabling process. A seemingly small incident is often just one of many dozens that occur routinely. All of these incidents weave an intricate web of enabling.

The story of Bill and Mark illustrates a second important point. Identification of enabling in oneself is difficult. If a teacher or police officer accused Bill of poor judgment or of protecting his son, this father would probably deny their assertions, and he'd do so in good faith.

If enabling is so complex and hard to detect, then how can we discover our own patterns? Three basic aspects of our personalities (feelings, beliefs, and behaviors) color our relationships with young people. By examining them, we can develop a greater awareness of how we unwittingly enable young people.

Feelings that Contribute to Enabling

Guilt. Guilt is a powerful feeling. In the story, Bill felt guilty about his divorce. This guilt played a key role in why he continually enabled Mark to be irresponsible.

Over-Protectiveness. Feeling protective of young people is normal for adults. A teacher might fail to report a star athlete for using alcohol at a school dance because the teacher doesn't want to jeopardize the student's eligibility. While the protective impulse can be helpful, it may also provide reasons to insulate young people from the consequences of their behavior.

Fear. Remember the story of the police officer in Chapter Two? The officer had witnessed numerous cases of family violence. When he discovered the three ninth graders drinking in the park, they pleaded with him not to tell their parents. The officer wasn't sure about the parents. If they were notified, would they hurt the youngsters?

The police officer decided instead to give the kids one more chance. He poured out the beer and sent them home. Fear is powerful. Fear for others provides us with what seems a noble motivation for enabling kids to use alcohol.

Beliefs that Contribute to Enabling

Kids listen only to other kids. They won't listen to what I say because I'm an adult. Nothing could be further from the truth. Young people often resort to outrageous and desperate behavior primarily to get adult attention. Young people are looking for and need our mature response and validation, especially as they make decisions related to alcohol and other drugs.

The most important source of adult validation is a young person's parents. Young people who do not use alcohol or other drugs say that a very important reason for not using is their concern about upsetting their parents (see Fact 3 on page 14).

Kids can't be responsible for themselves. They experience too much pressure. Young people today do face heavier pressures to use alcohol, smoke cigarettes, and be sexually active than kids in earlier generations. Peer pressure, media pressure, even athlete role models often present an image of success or independence that seems rooted in the brand of beer we drink or the type of cigarette we smoke.

However, these pressures don't excuse irresponsible behavior. If we excuse a young person's alcohol use because the teenager's adult role models engage in destructive acts, then we imply that we expect nothing more from our youngsters. *When we excuse behavior rather than help kids overcome obstacles, we enable them to be irresponsible.*

If everyone else is drinking, then drinking must be okay. Most of us deny buying into this belief, but this primary assumption underlies the enabling of underage alcohol use. Sometimes this belief takes a different form; for instance, we say, "I did the same thing when I was a kid" or "Boys will be boys."

The bottom line is that alcohol use is the number-one health hazard among young people today. If we believe drinking is acceptable because so many young people do it, then we become part of the problem. That is enabling in its most basic form.

Behaviors that Contribute to Enabling

Making Excuses. Sarah, a social worker, knew John was at high risk for developing problems with alcohol and other drugs: his dad was alcoholic, his mom had abandoned him, and recently, he had been living in a foster home. When the foster parents reported that John had been drinking, Sarah's response was that no one should be surprised—after all, look at the boy's history.

Granted, John has numerous obstacles to overcome. When Sarah used his history to excuse his behavior, however, she communicated to John and his foster parents that she had given up on him. Making excuses for young people's behavior actually enables them to be irresponsible.

Failing to Enforce the Law. Jerry is a checker at the local convenience store. Last night, a couple of kids tried to buy beer with a fake ID. Even though he knew the ID was fake, Jerry let the kids buy the six-pack anyway. After all, he's not a police officer; why should he try to make sure that everyone obeys the law?

In addition to the responsibility of shared concern for teenagers, many adults have a legal liability. In most states, adults who knowingly sell alcohol to underage young people can be charged and possibly held financially responsible for any consequences of this behavior.

Being a Friend Instead of Being an Adult. Susan was a second-year teacher. At the age of twenty-five, and only two years out of college, her adolescence wasn't too far from her memory. When two girls from her fifth-hour class told her about drinking wine coolers after last Friday's game, she didn't know how to react. She had worked hard to develop a relationship with these students, and she didn't want to jeopardize their friendship by sounding like a parent. She chose to say nothing.

Young people interpret a failure to respond as a sign of approval for what they tell an adult. While relating to young people "on their level" can help build a relationship, we must always remember that adults have a responsibility to be more than a peer.

Keeping Secrets. Helen had caught her thirteen-year-old son, Jamie, and his best friend sneaking two cans of beer from the refrigerator to take out to their tree fort. She knew that her husband would be furious if he found out, so she decided not to tell him. She stipulated one condition to her son: Jamie must promise never to sneak beer again.

Keeping some secrets can be wholesome fun: a surprise birthday party, an unexpected weekend getaway. But other secrets, such as Jamie's self-destructive action, become the foundation of enabling.

Shielding from Consequences. Interference with consequences teaches young people two powerful lessons: they are above the law or the rules, and someone will always bail them out of their problems. This was demonstrated in the vignette about Bill and Mark at the beginning of the chapter. When Bill hired an attorney to help Mark avoid the legal consequences of his alcohol use, he enabled Mark to continue his irresponsible behavior.

Our Own Enabling

Let's take some time now to reflect on how we sometimes enable the young people with whom we live or work.

1. I enable when I _____

   _____

   The reason I enable is that _____

   _____

2. I enable when I _____

   _____

   The reason I enable is that _____

   _____

3. I enable when I _____

   _____

   The reason I enable is that _____

   _____

4. I enable when I _____

   _____

   The reason I enable is that _____

   _____

5. I enable when I _____

   _____

   The reason I enable is that _____

   _____

Summary

Enabling has such power to harm because it is motivated by good will and we are usually not conscious of its destructiveness. As we consider the casualties of underage drinking, we adults must reflect on our own role in this critical issue.

If we are to have any impact on reversing the problem of underage alcohol use, then each of us must firmly consider how we have enabled this problem to continue.

What can we do? We must take the steps to *understand* enabling, to *identify* our own enabling characteristics, and to *admit* unflinchingly what we have done. Only after taking these three steps can we stop enabling young people. We can then empower them to be responsible.

What Parents Can Do

4

This fishing trip was especially satisfying to Ben. For the first time, his sixteen-year-old son, Tom, came along with the guys. Seeing Tom act like an adult had pleased Ben. Tom had handled himself well, especially when he brought in a six-pound bass. The only troubling incident occurred last night when the group had gathered around the campfire.

Joe had brought out a six-pack of beer and handed a can to each of them. Ben was shocked when Tom took one, and even more when he began drinking it. Ben suspected he should have said something, but he hadn't wanted to embarrass his son. Several thoughts had leaped into his mind: Tom had done so well on the fishing trip; he has acted like an adult. He's really beginning to seem like one of the guys. Maybe letting him have a drink is okay just this once. After all, this is a special occasion.

With these thoughts in mind, Ben had decided not to say anything.

Assessing Ben's Story

Parenthood poses continual challenges. Decisions about kids and alcohol can be especially confusing. Ben wants to do what he believes is the best thing for his son. Like many of us, however, he is caught in a painful contradiction.

On the one hand, he wants to reinforce the fact that Tom is growing up, that he has developed some of the skills of an adult. For Ben's buddies, a six-pack around the campfire in the evening is part of the ritual of a fishing trip. And Ben wants Tom to participate as a full-fledged adult member. After all, Tom paid his dues—he set up camp and caught a fish—and he deserved to be treated like one of the guys.

On the other hand, Tom is only sixteen. On Monday morning he'll be on the school bus as a sophomore in high school. Ben would be extremely upset if he heard that Tom had been drinking with friends after a ballgame. But here, sitting around the campfire, the situation seems different.

This story demonstrates just a part of the dilemma that we parents face regarding alcohol use and adolescents. The answers aren't foolproof, nor are they necessarily easy to arrive at. However, many parents have learned, sometimes the hard way, how to navigate through these tricky currents.

Seven Practical Actions

The following actions are practical guidelines for parents who struggle with the issue of alcohol use by adolescents.

1 We can set clear, non-negotiable limits regarding alcohol use by young people.

By saying nothing when Tom accepted a beer and drank it, Ben negotiated his rule about alcohol and other drugs. Ben thinks that Tom will recognize the difference between this beer around the campfire and a beer behind the bleachers with his friends. Tom won't. Without a word, Ben has communicated to his son that underage alcohol use is okay.

The consequences of this idea can be deadly. Negotiation of the rules occurs with verbal or nonverbal messages that imply "It's okay to use alcohol as long as you don't drink and drive" or "It's okay to use alcohol as long as you're with adults." Research shows that when parents negotiate limits, a teenager is significantly more likely to

- develop a serious problem with alcohol or other drugs
- drive or ride in a car driven by someone who has been drinking or using other drugs.[1]

A non-negotiable, no-use rule about alcohol may be difficult to talk about and sometimes socially awkward for a teenager. Even so, it is the best and simplest safeguard we can give our kids.

We parents must learn the skills and develop the confidence that help us speak up. Ben could have stepped in on the fishing trip without sacrificing the adult status that Tom was enjoying by saying or doing the following:

(1) Ben could have said, in a joking way, "Even though you out-fished some of the old timers in the group, Tom, certain privileges will have to wait."

(2) When the other men lugged out the cooler, Ben might have pulled Tom aside and reminded him that the cooler had soft drinks in it as well as beer and that even at camp the rule about alcohol use still stands.

(3) Ben could have silently signaled to Tom that taking a beer was not okay. Many parents develop non-verbal communication signals that sometimes speak louder than words.

The key point to remember is that no matter what the situation, we parents must stand by and enforce our rules regarding alcohol and other drugs.

2 We can follow through with consequences.

One of parents' primary jobs is to set limits. It is the nature of kids to test those limits.

Thus, most kids test even the clearest prohibitions, and parents often eventually find out. When we find that our children have used alcohol or other drugs we must respond. Some of the key points in establishing effective consequences are the following:

- The goal of consequences is education, not revenge or justice. We must *always* think about how and what the consequence will teach the child.

- Natural consequences work best. If the young person used alcohol during a social outing, for instance, loss of a social outing in the near future is a natural consequence.

- Consequences should affect the young person more than the parent. We need to choose a consequence that does not require us to be police officers indefinitely. Groundings that go on for weeks or months typically affect us and our own lives more than they do our kids.

- Consequences are most effective when we set them calmly. When a police officer sneers or yells or admonishes us as if we were small children, in addition to writing a ticket, we don't develop better driving habits. We focus instead on the person who made us feel so inadequate. Young people react the same way. When we yell or sneer or become sarcastic or, worse yet, hit, they learn very little about themselves or their own decisions. Instead, they concentrate all of their frustration on us.

(See Chapter 3 of *Parenting for Prevention,* published by Johnson Institute, for more in-depth details on setting consequences.)

3 We can talk about alcohol and other drugs early.

We can't wait until middle school to begin talking about alcohol and other drugs. Nor can we assume that our children are learning everything they need to know from school prevention programs. Even though schools are doing more than ever before, the research proves that kids who get alcohol and other drug information from parents are less likely to develop problems with use.[2]

We also need to remember that one discussion isn't enough. We must be comfortable enough with the topic of alcohol both to teach our kids and to learn from them about this vital topic throughout their school years.

4 We must take alcohol use seriously.

A long time has passed since an audience thought that Forest Brooks's or Dean Martin's drunk routines were funny. We now know that far from being funny, public displays of inappropriate alcohol or other drug use are dangerous.

Unfortunately, the media continues to bombard young people with inaccurate messages about alcohol. When students were questioned about their response to advertisements for alcoholic beverages, the most common answers pointed out that the ads spotlight attractive people and make drinking look like fun:

- The ads make drinking look glamorous.
- They make drinkers look exciting and fun.
- They suggest that people look cool and accepted when they drink.
- Girls in the alcohol ads are thin, and teenagers want to be like that.[3]

Kids look to their parents for accurate information. Explaining the media's inaccurate messages about alcohol can be the most important drug education possible for our kids.

Here's an activity parents and kids can do together. List T.V. commercials or cut out magazine ads for alcohol and mount them on paper. Alongside each ad, list the benefit communicated to the reader or listener. Some of the benefits often portrayed include attractiveness, masculinity, and athletic prowess. Finally, discuss whether the claimed benefits actually result from drinking alcohol.

5 We can work with other parents.

One of the primary reasons that we parents compromise with our kids regarding alcohol is the kids' insistence, "But all the other parents let their kids drink beer!" Although we may feel alone, the fact is that most parents are not comfortable with underage drinking.

One of the best ways for parents to feel empowered to take a firm stand is to form a parents' network. One successful network in Minnesota, Parents' Communication Network (PCN), was started by Sue Blaszczak of Apple Valley, Minnesota. She established informal ground rules for parent members that focused on three basic expectations:

- We will establish a no-use policy for all underage kids in our household.

- We will allow our kids to attend only adult-chaperoned parties at which alcohol or other drug use is prohibited.

- We will support other parents by maintaining open communication regarding our concerns for our children.

Many communities around the United States have helped parents to feel strong and secure in taking a stand against underage alcohol use by establishing parent communication networks that result in feelings of solidarity and support with other parents.

6 We can establish clear guidelines for parties.

Adolescence means parties. Teenagers need the social experience, but parties can be extremely dangerous for them if we do not establish clear rules. The Mounds View School District Parents' Communication Network in Minnesota has graciously permitted the reprinting of their practical ideas for teenage parties:

Guidelines for Parents of Teenagers Hosting a Party

Before the party...

1. *Set ground rules with your teenager.* Teens need to know what you expect, and you need to be aware of their feelings and concerns. Remember that subsequent parties should be easier once you have agreed to the basic rules.

2. *Share responsibility for hosting the party with your teen—no parents, no party!* Ask other parents to help you supervise. Take this opportunity to meet and get to know your teen's friends and their parents.

3. *Decide which part of the house will be used for the party.* Choose an area where guests will be comfortable and where you can maintain supervision and monitor entrances and exits. Do not allow guests to leave and return.

4. *Limit party attendance and times.* Be aware that large groups and open-hour parties make maintaining control difficult for you. Remember that other parents will appreciate time limits that enable teens to be home at a reasonable time before curfew.

5. *To discourage uninvited guests, make a guest list.* Do not allow party crashing.

6. *Encourage your teen to organize activities that will involve everyone and keep the party lively.*

7. *Have plenty of food and nonalcoholic drinks available.* Explain why minors should not drink and use other drugs. Let your teen know that you disapprove of any use. Be aware that clear family policies help teens say no to alcohol and other drugs.

8. *Understand state and local laws regarding alcohol and other drugs.* Be aware that offering alcohol to guests under the legal drinking age or allowing guests to use other illicit drugs in your home or on your property is illegal. You may be brought to court on criminal charges and you may have to pay monetary damages in a civil lawsuit if you furnish alcohol or other drugs to minors.

9. *Notify your neighbors that you are having a party.* Encourage your teen to call or send a note telling neighbors about the party.

10. *If you encounter any problems, notify the police.* Be aware that this will help protect you, your guests, and your neighbors. If necessary, discuss a plan for guest parking.

During the party...

1. *Be a responsible host.* Make sure to be available and to actively supervise the entire party. For instance, you might go in and out with snacks.

2. *Greet guests at the door when they arrive.* Ask another adult to supervise at the door during the party.

3. *Do not allow guests to come and go.* Do not allow anyone who leaves the party to return. Note that this discourages teens from leaving to drink or use other drugs and then return to the party.

4. *Notify the parents of teenagers who arrive at the party drunk to ensure their safe transportation home.* Do not let anyone drive under the influence of alcohol or other drugs, even if this means taking the keys and calling a cab or asking a sober adult to give the teenager a ride home. If a teen is out of control and the parents cannot be reached, call the police.

5. *Be prepared to ask guests to leave if they try to bring in alcohol or other drugs or are otherwise uncooperative.* Notify their parents.

6. *Be willing to call the police if unwanted guests refuse to leave or if loud music or disruptive behavior gets out of hand despite your precautions.*

7. *Be alert to signs of alcohol or other drug use by teenagers during the party.* Notify their parents.

8. *Be aware of behavior being modeled by the adults at functions where both adults and teenagers are present.* Remember that parents are important role models and that they influence the drinking patterns of teens. Consider serving only nonalcoholic beverages to adult chaperones.

9. *Replenish snacks and nonalcoholic drinks frequently.* Be aware that your intermittent presence will help keep the party running smoothly and will allow you to meet your teen's friends.

Guidelines for Parents of Teenagers Attending a Party

1. *Know where your teenager will be.* Obtain the name and phone number of the partygiver and the location of the party. Keep track of where your teen is going, with whom, and when he or she will be home. Let your teen know you expect a phone call before she or he goes somewhere else.

2. *Contact the parents of the partygiver and do the following:*

   • Verify the occasion.

   • Verify that a parent will be supervising.

   • Verify that the parent will not permit alcohol or other drugs.

   • Inquire about planned (and unplanned) activities.

   • Offer assistance.

3. *Know how your teenager will get to and from the party.* Assure your teen that you or a specific friend or neighbor can be called for a ride home. Make sure your teen has a quarter and the appropriate phone number(s). Discuss with your teen the possible situations when such a call might be made.

4. *Discuss with your teenager how to handle a situation in which alcohol or other drugs are available at a party.* Set firm guidelines against illegal drinking. Discuss these guidelines regularly and clarify any misconceptions your teenager has about them. Specify which behaviors are not permitted. Don't assume your teen knows the rules. Help your teen come up with acceptable ways to refuse alcohol or other drugs. Do this by role playing or by discussing ways other teens have handled this situation.

5. *Make sure your teenager knows what time to be home, keeping legal curfew limits in mind.* Do not allow the rules to change between the times you have established them and the time your teen arrives home. In other words, allow no manipulations.

6. *Be awake, ask your teen to awaken you, or set your alarm for when your teen is due home.* Remember that this is often a good time for sharing. Be alert to signs of drinking or other drug use.

7. *Have your teenager contact you before agreeing to spend the night with a friend after a party.* Be aware that sleeping-over is a classic way to avoid the consequences of a drinking incident. Insist that your teenager confirm spontaneous sleep-over arrangements with the host parents. Verify with the parents that they want your teen to stay, that they will be home, and that you are in agreement on curfew hours and other basic house rules.

8. *Suggest that your teenager phone or write the partygivers the next day to thank them for hosting the party.* You may want to phone the parents to thank them, too.

7 We can model responsible choices.

We've all had the experience of being upset about kids' behavior only to be reminded that the apple didn't fall far from the tree. A truism we often hear is that our kids learn more from what we do than from what we say.

One of the immediate questions parents ask is, "Isn't telling my sixteen-year-old that she can't drink a double message when she knows that her stepfather has an occasional glass of wine?"

The answer is no, this is not a double message. Government and communities routinely put age limits on many activities that require a certain level of responsibility or can be potentially dangerous, such as driving a car, having a credit card, voting, piloting a plane, holding public office, entering the armed services, and so on. The use of alcohol is potentially dangerous. Consequently, limiting its use to adults of a specific age is clearly logical.

Even though our culture considers alcohol legal for adults, the example we set in the way we use this potentially dangerous drug is critical. We must model behavior that does not communicate the following false messages to our kids:

- *The only way to relax is with a drink.* When we always associate relaxation with alcohol, we convey this dangerous message.

- *Adults have fun only when they drink.* We must avoid falling into the pattern of serving alcohol at every adult get-together to avoid this inadvertent message.

- *The best way to deal with stress or pressure is to drink.* The stress of work, divorce, separation, and so on may lead to excessive use of alcohol. While the dangers of this type of use can be destructive for us as individuals, the implications carry even far greater harm for our kids.

- *All adults drink.* Many adults choose not to drink for a variety of reasons. Young people need to be reminded that even though the media and others might suggest that all adults use alcohol, many of us choose not to. Abstinence from alcohol should always be presented as a realistic and positive choice for adults.

Our behavior gives kids a message that is much louder than words. Sometimes we are the last to understand what our actions say to other people. Other adults who know us well can give us insight into the messages our behavior communicates to young people.

What Schools Can Do

5

Rosa Juarez teaches English at the high school. The first week of every month she monitors the girls' bathroom on her wing of the school. Yesterday she walked in on two sophomore girls sharing sips from a bottle. She knew they were drinking alcohol. When she confronted the two and asked what they were doing, the girl with the bottle slid it back into her purse. The two sophomores responded with the routine, "Nothing," and scurried out of the bathroom.

Ms. Juarez knew these girls. One was in her fifth-hour, the other in her second-hour class. They were both conscientious students. If she reported the incident, she was afraid they would get in trouble. One of the girls, who played on the basketball team, would surely lose her eligibility if Ms. Juarez reported the incident. So she decided to pretend that she had seen nothing. After all, these were good kids. She was sure they would never sneak alcohol again.

Once again, as we have seen in other examples of enabling throughout this book, Rosa Juarez's good intention has resulted in a destructive message for her students. By pretending that she saw nothing, Ms. Juarez becomes a part of the enabling system within the school.

As our culture becomes increasingly mobile and fragmented, the school is proportionally more important in providing for the needs of the whole child. In today's culture, students in the third and fourth grades are making alcohol and other drug use choices. A survey done by *Weekly Reader* in 1990 indicates that 34 percent of fourth graders feel "some" to "a lot" of peer pressure to use wine coolers. We must mobilize to deal with this crisis in a firm but positive way. The positive response of the school to this critical issue is essential if we are to clearly communicate our concern to young people.

To establish an educational atmosphere that appropriately addresses issues of underage drinking, schools can take the following actions:

Schools can establish a policy that is uniformly enforced. One of the primary issues in many schools is that while policies exist, the staff does not enforce them. Some typical reasons that educators offer for the failure to enforce policies related to underage drinking are the following:

- They aren't sure what the rules are.
- They believe the rules are too punitive.
- They get caught up in enabling alcohol use.
- They believe the administration will not effectively follow through with consequences.
- They fear retaliation from students, parents, or community.

While school policies vary from state to state and district to district, the following key policy characteristics recommended by the U.S. Department of Education are essential considerations in school policy regarding student use of alcohol or other drugs:

- Establish clear and specific rules regarding alcohol and other drug use that include strong corrective actions.

School policies should clearly establish that drug use, possession, and sale on the school grounds and at school functions will not be tolerated. These policies should apply both to students and to school personnel, and may include prevention, intervention, treatment, and disciplinary measures.

- Specify what constitutes a drug offense by defining illegal substances and paraphernalia; the area of the school's jurisdiction (for example, the school property, its surroundings, and all school-related events, such as proms and football games); and the types of violations (drug possession, use, and sale).

- State the consequences for violating school policy: link punitive action to referral for treatment and counseling. Measures that schools have found effective in dealing with first-time offenders include the following:

  - A required meeting of parents and the student with school officials, concluding with a contract signed by the student and parents in which they both acknowledge a drug problem and the student agrees to stop using and to participate in drug counseling or a rehabilitation program.

  - Suspension, assignment to an alternative school, in-school suspension, after-school or Saturday detention with close supervision, and demanding academic assignments.

  - Referral to a drug treatment expert or counselor.

  - Notification of police.

- Penalties for repeat offenders and for sellers may include expulsion, legal action, and referral for treatment.

  - Legal issues associated with disciplinary actions (confidentiality, due process, and search and seizure) and their application.

- – Circumstances under which incidents should be reported and the responsibilities and procedures for reporting incidents, including the identification of the authorities to be contacted.

- – Procedures for notifying parents when their child is suspected of using drugs or is caught with drugs.

- – Procedures for notifying police.

- Enlist legal counsel to ensure that all policy is in compliance with applicable federal, state, and local laws.

- Build community support for the policy. Hold open meetings where views can be aired and differences resolved.[1]

Schools can establish a student assistance program. The goal of the student assistance program (SAP) is to help educators like Rosa Juarez deal constructively with the situation she encountered in the restroom with her students.

Student assistance programs:

- Keep educators updated on how to identify alcohol and other drug use and how to report it.

- Screen referrals made by teachers and other staff to assure that these referrals are handled appropriately and consistently.

- Notify and involve parents when students with alcohol or other drug use problems are identified.

- Follow through with ongoing support and monitoring of students who have been identified as potentially having a problem with alcohol or other drugs.

The student assistance program in Northside School district in San Antonio, Texas, provides an example of a successful SAP and shows how it works.

Marcia Loew, a guidance counselor, was recruited as the SAP coordinator. Her first step was to begin the process of training the staff. They would need skills in order to develop a program in her school. She established a core team made up of the school nurse, assistant principal, a health teacher, and herself. The goal of the core team was to advise and review cases with her. Then Marcia trained the rest of the faculty and staff. They learned the clues that identify a student who might be in trouble with alcohol or other drug use.

Shortly after the inservice, one student was identified and referred by five different staff people. Jerry (a fictitious name) showed all the tell-tale behaviors. He was consistently truant. He often failed to complete assignments. His defiance to teachers disrupted classes. And his grades were so poor that he was repeating the ninth grade.

When Marcia requested a conference, she let Jerry know that the information he told her was confidential. She would violate his confidentiality only if he indicated an intention to harm someone else or himself. During the first meeting, he revealed that he occasionally used alcohol and marijuana, but claimed that neither drug was a problem. Marcia also discovered that his two older siblings were in jail, and that his father had been shot and killed when Jerry was an infant.

Marcia suggested that he attend the group that she was forming for students who had been identified as drug users. He refused. Marcia also requested permission to contact his mother. He again refused, but he did agree to meet with Marcia again. During the second meeting, Jerry agreed to attend the group. Marcia reported that his involvement in group consisted primarily of one-upmanship. He risked very little, but he did continue to attend.

By the end of early spring, Jerry seemed to be making some progress. He regularly attended group, and his school attendance and grades were improving. Nevertheless, Marcia was still concerned. She consulted her core team because she felt that Jerry needed more help than she could possibly provide. However, she knew the family had no insurance or resources for treatment or outside counseling. Also, Jerry still refused to allow her to contact his mother.

Suddenly, in early May, Jerry quit coming to school. The rumor around the building was that he was going to drop out at the age of seventeen. Marcia heard nothing more from him until the following year. That fall, Jerry came to school to register. Because of his age and his problems the previous year, the administration was reluctant to allow him to enroll.

Marcia met with Jerry and his mother. She established a contract that he agreed to sign, stipulating that Jerry would attend school every day and continue in group. Jerry's performance in school consistently improved. He maintained the contract with only minimal problems.

As Jerry became more honest about his problem with alcohol and other drugs and his desire to get sober, Marcia suggested that he begin attending the abstinence group of students who were chemically dependent and supporting each other in their efforts to stay sober.

He began the new group, but had problems fitting in. Marcia heard rumors that he had started using again. Finally he returned to the group and began establishing a few connections with sober peers. At Marcia's suggestion, although he had refused to cooperate on her previous suggestions, he agreed to be tested for a possible learning disability. As a result, he was identified as eligible for special education classes.

Five months into the new year, Marcia says that Jerry looks like a different student. His hair is no longer multihued, and he's dressing like other students. Even the spiked bracelets are gone. She also reports that his smile seems genuine. His skin has lost its former ashen pallor. Jerry currently receives remedial instruction to develop his basic skills to grade level. He has been sober for over four months and intends to graduate.

Without a student assistance program and the supportive nurturance of a professional like Marcia Loew, Jerry was likely to become just another casualty of the system. Students like Jerry can be helped. The key is to establish a student assistance program in every building that will keep the "Jerrys" from falling through the cracks.

Schools can establish alcohol and other drug prevention programs within the school curricula. Effective prevention curricula must cover more than just facts about alcohol and other drugs. Research shows that when information is presented simultaneously with activities that help students learn how to use the information, then we have greatly enhanced the prevention effort.

An effective drug prevention curriculum implements a broad set of education objectives which are outlined in greater detail in the Department of Education's handbook, *Drug Prevention Curricula: A Guide to Selection and Implementation.* The Department's model program consists of four objectives plus sample topics and learning activities. They are reprinted in part on the remaining pages in this chapter.

Objective 1. To value and maintain sound personal health; to understand how drugs affect health.

An effective drug prevention education program instills respect for a healthy body and mind and imparts knowledge of how the body functions, how personal habits contribute to good health, and how drugs affect the body.

At the early elementary level, children learn how to take care of their bodies. Knowledge about habits, medicine, and poisons lays the foundation for learning about drugs. Older children begin to learn about the drug problem and study those drugs to which they are most likely to be exposed. The curriculum for secondary school students is increasingly drug-specific as students learn about the effects of drugs on their bodies and on adolescent maturation. Health consequences of drug use, including transmission of AIDS, are emphasized.

Sample topics for elementary school:

- The roles of nutrition, medicine, and health care professionals in preventing and treating disease.
- The difficulties of recognizing which substances are safe to eat, drink, or touch; ways to learn whether a substance is safe by consulting with an adult and by reading labels.
- The effects of poisons on the body; the effects of medicine on body chemistry: the wrong drug may make a person ill.
- The nature of habits: their conscious and unconscious development.

Sample topics for secondary school:

- Stress: how the body responds to stress; how drugs increase stress.
- The chemical properties of drugs.
- The effects of drugs on body systems. The effects of drugs on adolescent development.
- Patterns of alcohol and other drug abuse: the progressive effects of drugs on the body and mind.
- What is addiction?
- How to get help for a drug or alcohol problem.

Objective 2.   To respect laws and rules prohibiting drugs.

The program teaches children to respect rules and laws as the embodiment of social values and as tools for protecting individuals and society. It provides specific instruction about laws concerning drugs.

Students in the early grades learn to identify rules and to understand their importance, while older students learn about the school drug code and laws regarding alcohol and other drugs.

Sample topics for elementary school:

- What rules are and what would happen without them.

- What values are and why they should guide behavior.

- What responsible behavior is.

- Why it is wrong to take drugs.

Sample topics for secondary school:

- Student responsibilities in promoting a drug-free school.

- Local, state, and federal laws on controlled substances; why these laws exist and how they are enforced.

- Legal consequences of drug use; penalties for driving under the influence of alcohol or other drugs; the relationship between drugs and crime.

- Personal and societal costs of drug use.

Objective 3.   To recognize and resist pressures to use drugs.

Social influences play a key role in encouraging children to try alcohol and other drugs. Pressures to use drugs come from internal sources, such as a child's desire to feel included in a group or to demonstrate independence, and external influences, such as the opinions and example of friends, older children and adults, and media messages.

Students must learn to identify these pressures. They must then learn how to counteract messages to use alcohol and other drugs and gain practice in saying no. The education program emphasizes influences on behavior, responsible decision making, and techniques for resisting pressures to use drugs.

Sample topics for elementary through high school:

- The influence of popular culture on behavior.
- The influence of peers, parents, and other important individuals on a student's behavior; ways in which the need to feel accepted by others influences behavior.
- Ways to make responsible decisions and to deal constructively with disagreeable moments and pressures.
- Reasons for not taking drugs.
- Situations in which students may be pressured into using alcohol and other drugs.
- Ways of resisting pressure to use drugs.
- Effects of drug use on family and friends, and benefits of resisting pressure to use drugs.

Objective 4. To promote activities that reinforce the positive, drug-free elements of student life.

School activities that provide opportunities for students to have fun without alcohol and other drugs, and to contribute to the school community, build momentum for peer pressure not to use alcohol and other drugs. These school activities also nurture positive examples by giving older students opportunities for leadership related to drug prevention.

Sample activities:

- Make participation in school activities dependent on an agreement not to use alcohol and other drugs.

- Ensure that alcohol and other drugs will not be available at school-sponsored activities or parties. Plan these events carefully to be certain that students have attractive alternatives to drug use.

- Give students opportunities for leadership. They can be trained to serve as peer leaders in drug prevention programs, to write plays, or to design posters for younger students. Activities such as these provide youthful role models who demonstrate the importance of not using drugs. Youth training programs are available that prepare students to assist in drug education and provide information on how to form drug-free youth groups.

- Form action teams for school improvement with membership limited to students who are drug free. These action teams campaign against drug use, design special drug-free events, conduct and follow up on surveys of school needs, help teachers with paperwork, tutor other students, or improve the appearance of the school. Through these activities, students develop a stake in their school, have the opportunity to serve others, and have positive reasons to reject drug use.

- Survey community resources that offer help for alcohol or other drug problems or ways to cope with drug use by a family member.

- Create a program in the school for support of students returning from treatment.[2]

Schools can establish benchmark measurements to continue evaluating the effectiveness of prevention efforts. Most schools routinely test students to monitor the effectiveness of math, reading, and geography programs. Unfortunately, too few schools routinely measure the outcome of their prevention efforts.

The U.S. Department of Education recommends that schools "determine the extent and character of alcohol and other drug use and monitor that use regularly."[3] One of the methods the Department recommends is to "conduct anonymous surveys of students and school personnel and consult with local law enforcement officials to identify the extent of the problem."

Johnson Institute has developed a survey instrument called *StudentView*® to assist educators in this task. *StudentView*® is designed not only to help define the extent of the problem but also to help schools focus their prevention efforts. By using such a survey on an ongoing basis, educators can begin to assess the impact of their student assistance programs and their prevention efforts.

Schools play a critical role in both prevention of alcohol use problems among young people and intervention when they occur. However, educators cannot solve the problem on their own. Too often we want to dump responsibility on the education system for problems with roots in our families and in our communities. Only by linking parents, schools, and the larger community can we hope to make a difference.

Schools can dismantle the system of enabling. For a variety of reasons, Rosa Juarez enabled her two students. Most importantly, however, she didn't want to cause problems for them.

Enabling is a natural instinct that is almost always motivated by the best of intentions. The only way that educators will stop enabling is if each school does the following:

- Provides the staff with regular training that focuses specifically on how to help someone who uses alcohol or other drugs. This includes helping the staff become aware of their own and others' enabling behaviors and showing them ways to change that behavior.

- Helps staff members clearly understand their role in enforcing school policy regarding alcohol and other drugs.

- Makes clear to the staff that the school has established its policy and its student assistance program in order to *help*, not *hurt* students.

What Communities Can Do

6

Dateline: May 22, 1992. Senior Skip Day had been on the high school social calendar for the past six months. They had organized bake sales, car washes, and assorted other projects to raise money for the big party planned for the coming spring.

The night before the event, a seventeen-year-old student ordered sixteen kegs of beer for the party. On the morning of Senior Skip Day, that student and his grandmother picked up the kegs. The party began around 11 A.M., attended by approximately two hundred underage students. Most of the recreation revolved around the sixteen kegs of beer.

By late afternoon, as younger students from school joined in the festivities, someone accused a lower-classman of drinking beer he hadn't paid for. A fight broke out, and someone pulled a gun. Two kids were killed: a stray bullet killed a fifteen-year-old; a seventeen-year-old senior died from another bullet wound.

How Could This Disaster Happen?

An investigation into the death of the two teenagers revealed several shocking facts:

- A grandparent had called the police and the sheriff's department two days before the event. He was worried that someone would get hurt because of underage drinking. Both the police and sheriff departments did nothing. One department denies receiving the call, and members of the other said that they couldn't do anything about the situation.

- Almost all of the parents knew that underage drinking would occur at this event. They not only allowed the event, they also permitted their children to participate. Some parents reportedly participated in the fundraising for the beer.

- When the police arrived at the scene of the killings, all two hundred kids, most of whom had been drinking all day, drove their vehicles home, risking further casualties.

- The liquor store that took the order from the seventeen-year-old did not hesitate to sell sixteen kegs of beer to an underage person. Since then, the liquor store reportedly has lost its liquor license.

- At the scene of the killings, the police recovered numerous other bottles of hard liquor and five handguns from underage students.

- After the event, the majority of concern in the community focused primarily on violence and guns. The obvious issue of underage drinking was often ignored or minimized.

This story is disturbing not because it happened once in an eastern city, but because variations on this theme occur frequently in many communities across the nation. The consequences are not always as extreme or as dramatic as they were in this story, but often they are.

This true story makes clear that when a whole community— parents, teachers, police officers, businesses, the media, and so on— shrugs off adult responsibility regarding underage drinking, young people pay the price.

The story also illustrates that not only are schools, parents, and young people themselves responsible for the consequences of underage drinking, but that the responsibility belongs to all of us.

Communities are beginning to understand the role they play in preventing underage drinking, and they usually find that the most effective solutions are those that are developed, implemented, and managed by members of the community. Prevention programs that work always reflect the community's norms and standards.

Every community has different strengths and challenges. In order to make a real impact you will need to mobilize a variety of systems that cut across the entire community. Experience tells us that diverse community coalitions are usually at the foundation of the most successful prevention efforts.

The following questions use information from the U.S. Center for Substance Abuse Prevention as a way to start brainstorming on how to mobilize your community to act constructively.

The Legal System

YES   NO

1. Do police officers in my community enforce laws regarding underage drinking, or do they often overlook underage alcohol use by using "warn and release" enforcement methods?

    ____   ____

2. Do law enforcement officials actively participate in or sponsor prevention activities within my community?

    ____   ____

3. Do law enforcement officers have a positive working relationship with other youth-serving organizations, such as schools, court diversion programs, youth counselors, and so on?

    ____   ____

4. Are the fines and property collected from alcohol and other drug-related offenses used for prevention efforts?

    ____   ____

5. Are my state and federal elected officials aware of my own and my community's concerns regarding the problem of underage drinking?

    ____   ____

6. Does the juvenile court system enforce the law using consequences that have a real impact on the young person (loss of a driver's license, for example, rather than monetary fines which are often paid by parents)?

    ____   ____

7. Does my community assure that first-time underage drinkers who are arrested receive support and educational services as part of their legal consequences for drinking?

    ____   ____

The Business Community

YES   NO

8. Are bars, restaurants, and alcohol retailers in my community committed to stopping underage use of alcohol? ____ ____

9. Do bartenders, waiters, and retailers routinely check ID's of young adults? ____ ____

10. Are restaurants and retailers legally prosecuted when they sell alcohol to underage customers? ____ ____

11. Does my community sponsor training programs about underage drinking issues for servers and clerks who sell alcohol? ____ ____

12. Do the businesses in my community sponsor or support prevention programs that focus on alcohol use in the community? ____ ____

The Religious Community

YES   NO

13. Do religious leaders in my community take a public stand and speak out regarding underage use of alcohol? ____ ____

14. Do religious groups in my area have programs, a staff, or volunteers who are knowledgeable about intervention and prevention of alcohol and other drug problems? ____ ____

15. Do the religious groups incorporate prevention messages within their youth education programs? ____ ____

16. Do churches and synagogues donate space, equipment, or other resources to prevention groups within my community? ____ ____

17. Does the religious community offer education programs that teach parents skills to prevent underage drinking? ____ ____

The Health Care Community

YES NO

18. Are doctors, dentists, and pharmacists involved in the prevention efforts in my community? ____ ____

19. Do health care providers contribute their expertise as guest trainers and resources for others who need their expertise? ____ ____

20. Do health care providers in my community have access to ongoing training to assure that they know the latest information regarding treatment and prevention of chemical dependence? ____ ____

21. Do counseling or treatment programs exist for people who develop problems with alcohol or other drug use in my area? ____ ____

22. Do counseling or treatment programs sponsor activities to inform the public about alcohol and other drug use problems? ____ ____

Youth/Recreation Groups

YES NO

23. Do youth and recreation groups in my area have clear policies and guidelines regarding underage use of alcohol? ____ ____

24. Have coaches, youth leaders, and other staff members been trained to identify and assist young people who are using alcohol or other drugs? ____ ____

25. Do the recreation groups in my area incorporate prevention messages and skills into their activities? _____ _____

26. Do the programs have special services available for young people who have been identified "at risk" for alcohol or other drug use problems? _____ _____

Civic Organizations

YES   NO

27. Do civic or service organizations in my community include discussions about underage drinking on their agendas? _____ _____

28. Do these groups sponsor prevention activities that prevent underage alcohol use? _____ _____

29. Do these civic groups participate in special community prevention events or help raise funds to sponsor these events? _____ _____

Local Media

YES   NO

30. Do the hosts of radio or T.V. talk shows in my community discuss the problem of underage drinking on their programs? _____ _____

31. Do the local media provide public service messages or free advertising space for prevention messages or announcements? _____ _____

32. Do the local print media take a stand regarding underage use of alcohol in their editorial section? _____ _____

After reading through this list of ideas for community action, think about the ideas that you feel are most important. An activity targeting which issue would be the most likely to get results? Which activity would require more time and resources than you as an individual have at your disposal? As you answer these questions, you are beginning to form the foundation for an action plan. You can mobilize your community for prevention of underage use of alcohol.

To avoid burnout and frustration, start with one or two activities that you can complete within two to four weeks. Commit yourself to share your goal with three friends. As you achieve success with your first activities and share your success with your friends, you will have the beginnings of a Community Action Group. Continue to establish goals that will not only build your group but will make a difference in your community. As you grow and develop, you will find that many friends and neighbors are as concerned and committed as your are. Every community will mobilize to protect its children if given clear information, adequate support, and persistent leadership.

Conclusion

7

In the past five years, stories of drug use and the casualties it creates have filled our newspapers. The tragedies have devastated our society.

When we hear these stories of pain or suffering, we want to look for a faceless or foreign menace infiltrating our turf and inflicting the damage. Most recently, we have been tempted to focus all of our anger on drugs such as cocaine or crack. We have deceived ourselves that the location for the war on drugs was in far-off places like Colombia or Ecuador. Many of us have wanted to blame drug pushers, whom we typically define as members of races or cultures different from our own, who sneak into our schools and hook our kids on drugs.

The reality is, of course, considerably different from that scapegoating myth. The primary drug that our kids turn to is neither foreign nor mysterious—it is alcohol. It is not imported from South America—it comes from the local convenience store, supermarket, or gas station. The people who supply our children are not mysterious, either. Their suppliers are us. Too often we adults shrug off our responsibilities for drug use by young people. We blame the government, the public, the pushers, the schools, the peer group: anyone but ourselves.

The reality is that each of us—every one of us reading this book—has a personal relationship with young people who need our help. They need us to give them information. They need us to quit looking the other way. They need us to hold them accountable. They need us to take the time to guide them with tough choices. They need us to voice our beliefs in a quiet but firm way. They need us to be there with our love and wisdom, because if we don't—there's a very good chance that nobody else will.

Notes

Chapter 1: Introduction

1. *Healthy People 2000: National Health Promotion and Disease Prevention Objectives,* U.S. Department of Health and Human Services, 1991, 166.

2. "Alcohol Related Injuries and Violence," *Prevention Pipeline* 5(3), Center for Substance Abuse Prevention, May/June 1992, 4.

3. Ruth L. Berkelman, Joy L. Herndon, Naice L. Callway, Robert Stivers, et al., "Fatal Injuries and Alcohol," *American Journal of Preventive Medicine,* November/December 1985, 21-8.

4. Charlene L. Muehlenhard and Melaney A. Linton, "Date Rape and Sexual Aggression in Dating Situations: Incidence and Risk Factors," *Journal of Counseling Psychology,* 1987, 189-96.

5. Lee Strunin and Ralph Hingson, "Alcohol, Drugs, and Adolescent Sexual Behavior," *International Journal of the Addictions,* 3 February 1992, 129-46.

6. David A. Brent, Joshua A. Perper, and Christopher J. Allman, "Alcohol, Firearms, and Suicide Among Youth—Temporal Trends in Allegheny County, Pennsylvania, 1960-1983," *Journal of American Medical Association,* 26 June 1987, 3369-72.

7. Garen J. Wintemute, Jess F. Kraus, Stephen P. Teret, and Mona Wright, "Drowning in Childhood and Adolescence: A Population-Based Study," *American Journal of Public Health,* July 1987, 830-2; James P. Orlowski, "Adolescent Drownings: Swimming, Boating, Diving, and Scuba Accidents," *Pediatric Annals,* February 1987, 125-8, 131-2.

8. Carnegie Foundation for the Advancement of Teaching, *Campus Life in Search of Community,* 1990.

9. "Alcohol Related Injuries and Violence," 12.

10. *StudentView® Aggregate Survey Data of 15,000 Students,* Johnson Institute, 1993.

11. *Youth and Alcohol: A National Survey,* Office of the Inspector General, U.S. Department of Health and Human Services, 1991, 11.

12. "Drinking Habits, Access, Attitudes, and Knowledge," *Youth and Alcohol: A National Survey,* Office of the Inspector General, U.S. Department of Health and Human Services, June 1991, 11.

13. "Is the 21-Year-Old Drinking Age a Myth?" *Youth and Alcohol: Laws and Enforcement,* Office of the Inspector General, U.S. Department of Health and Human Services, 1991, 15.

14. *Youth and Drugs: Society's Mixed Messages,* Office of Substance Abuse Prevention, U.S. Department of Health and Human Services, Prevention Monograph 6, 1990, 80.

15. H.J. Harwood, D.M. Napolitana, P.L. Kristiansen, and J J. Collins, *Economic Costs to Society of Alcohol and Drug Abuse and Mental Illness: 1980,* Research Triangle Park, NC: Research Triangle Institute, 1984.

16. D.P. Rice, L.S. Kelman, and S. Dunmeyer, *The Economic Costs of Alcohol and Drug Abuse and Mental Illness,* San Francisco: Institute for Health and Aging, University of California—San Francisco, 1990.

17. "Is the 21-Year-Old Drinking Age a Myth?", 12.

18. K. Womble, "The Impact of Minimum Drinking Age Laws on Fatal Crash Involvements, An Update of the NHTSA Analysis," U.S. Department of Transportation, 1987, 1.

Chapter 2: Acting on Falsehoods

1. *StudentView® Aggregate Survey Data of 15,000 Students,* Johnson Institute, 1993.

2. Ibid.

3. "Drinking Habits, Access, Attitudes, and Knowledge," *Youth and Alcohol: A National Survey,* Office of the Inspector General, Department of Health and Human Services, 1991, 10-11.

Chapter 4: What Parents Can Do

1. *StudentView® Aggregate Survey Data of 15,000 Students,* Johnson Institute, 1993.

2. *Youth and Alcohol: A National Survey,* Office of the Inspector General, U.S. Department of Health and Human Services, 1991, 11.

3. Ibid., 14.

Chapter 5: What Schools Can Do

1. *What Works, Schools Without Drugs*, U.S. Department of Education, 1989, 23-24.

2. Ibid., 44-49.

3. Ibid., 21.

Resources

The following materials are just some of the valuable resources available from Johnson Institute:

> 7205 Ohms Lane
> Minneapolis, MN 55439-2159
> United States or Canada: 800-231-5165
> Minneapolis/St. Paul: 612-831-1630

Books

Anderson, Gary L. *Solving Alcohol/Drug Problems in Your School.*

————. *Enabling in the School Setting.*

Christensen, Linda. *You Can Make a Difference: Characteristics and Skills of the Effective Prevention Teacher.*

Cohen, Peter, R., M.D. *Helping Your Chemically Dependent Teenager Recover.*

Daley, Dennis C., and Judy Miller. *When Your Child Is Chemically Dependent.*

Fleming, Martin. *Conducting Support Groups for Students Affected by Chemical Dependence.*

Johnson, Vernon E., D.D. *Intervention: How to Help Someone Who Doesn't Want Help.*

Moe, Jerry, and Peter Ways, M.D. *Conducting Support Groups for Elementary Children K-6.*

Sassatelli, Jean. *Breaking Away: Saying Goodbye to Alcohol/Drugs—A Guide to Help Teenagers Stop Using Chemicals.*

Schaefer, Dick. *Choices & Consequences®: What to Do When a Teenager Uses Alcohol/Drugs.*

Spencer, Carol. *Parenting Alone: Raising Your Children After One Parent Leaves.*

_____. *When One Parent Leaves: Surviving the Loss without Alcohol and Other Drugs.*

Turning Troubled Kids Around: The Complete Student Assistance Program for Secondary Schools.

Wilmes, David, J. *Parenting for Prevention: How to Raise a Child to Say No to Alcohol/Drugs.*

_____. *Parenting for Prevention—A Parent Education Curriculum: Raising a Child to Say No to Alcohol and Other Drugs.*

Wilmes, David, J., and Dick Schaefer. *Resources for Parenting.* (12 booklets).

Zarek, David, and James Sipe. *Can I Handle Alcohol/Drugs?: A Self-Assessment Guide for Youth.*

Videos

Another Chance to Change: A Teenager's Struggle with Relapse and Recovery. Color, 30 minutes.

Choices & Consequences®: Intervention with Youth In Trouble with Alcohol/Drugs. Color, 33 minutes.

Different Like Me®: For Teenage Children of Alcoholics. Color, 31 minutes.

Good Intentions, Bad Results: A Story about Friends Who Learn That Enabling Hurts. Color, 30 minutes.

Kids at Risk: A Four-part Video Series for Middle School Children:
    Covering Up for Kevin. Color, 17 minutes.
    Blaming Kitty. Color, 18 minutes.
    An Attitude Adjustment for Ramie. Color, 15 minutes.
    Double Bind. Color, 15 minutes.

A Story About Feelings. Animated, Color, 10 minutes.

Tulip Doesn't Feel Safe. Animated, Color, 12 minutes.

Twee, Fiddle and Huff. Animated, Color, 16 minutes.

Where's Shelley? Color, 13 minutes.